Writing about Literature

A Hacker Handbooks Supplement

Diana Hacker

Nancy Sommers
Harvard University

Consulting Editor
Joseph Bizup
Boston University

BEDFORD / ST. MARTIN'S   BOSTON ◆ NEW YORK

Manufactured in the United States of America.

5   4   3   2   1   0
f   e   d   c   b   a

For information, write: Bedford/St. Martin's, 75 Arlington Street, Boston, MA 02116 (617-399-4000)

ISBN-10: 0-312-65684-X
ISBN-13: 978-0-312-65684-3

ACKNOWLEDGMENTS

Acknowledgments and copyrights can be found at the back of the book on pages L-55 and L-56, which constitute an extension of the copyright page. It is a violation of the law to reproduce these selections by any means whatsoever without the written permission of the copyright holder.

Writing about
Literature

L Writing about Literature

All good writing about literature attempts to answer a question, spoken or unspoken, about the text:

- Why does Hamlet hesitate for so long before killing his uncle, King Claudius?
- How does street language function in Gwendolyn Brooks's "We Real Cool"?
- What does Orwell's "Shooting an Elephant" imply about the role the British played in imperial India?
- What does the relationship between Hana and Kip in Michael Ondaatje's novel *The English Patient* suggest about love and nationality?
- What is the connection between Latin and Gaelic in Brian Friel's play *Translations*?
- Why does Margaret Atwood make so many biblical allusions in *The Handmaid's Tale*?
- In what ways does Louise Erdrich's *Love Medicine* draw on oral narrative traditions?
- Why does it matter that Robert Hayden's poem "Those Winter Sundays" is about winter Sundays (as opposed to, say, winter Tuesdays)?

The goal of a literature paper should be to address such questions with a meaningful interpretation, presented both forcefully and persuasively.

L1 Reading to form an interpretation

L1-a Get involved in the work; be an active reader.

Read the work through once, closely and carefully. Think of it as speaking to you: What is it telling you? Asking you? Trying to make you feel? Then go back and read it a second time. If the work provides an introduction and footnotes, read them attentively. They may be a source of important information. Use the dictionary to look up words that are unfamiliar to you or words with subtle nuances that may affect the work's meaning.

Rereading is a central part of the process of developing your interpretation. You should read short works several times, first to get an overall impression and then again to focus on meaningful details. With longer works, such as novels or plays, read the most important chapters or scenes more than once while keeping in mind the work as a whole.

As you read and reread, interact with the work by posing questions and looking for possible answers. The chart that begins on page L-8 suggests some questions about literature that may help you become a more active reader.

Annotating the work

Annotating the work is a way to focus your reading. If you own a copy of the work, you should feel free to make notes on it. If you do not, make a photocopy. The first time you read the work through, you may want to pencil a check mark next to passages you find especially significant. On a more careful rereading, pay particular attention to these passages and jot down your ideas and reactions in the margins of the page.

Here is one student's annotation of a poem by Shakespeare.

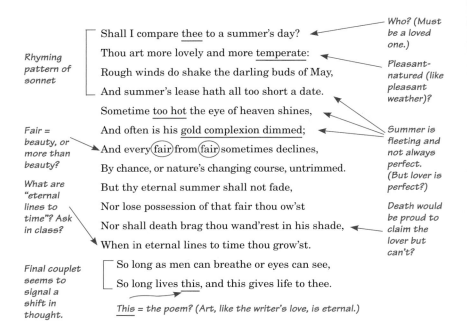

Rhyming pattern of sonnet

Shall I compare thee to a summer's day?
Thou art more lovely and more temperate:
Rough winds do shake the darling buds of May,
And summer's lease hath all too short a date.

Who? (Must be a loved one.)

Pleasant-natured (like pleasant weather)?

Sometime too hot the eye of heaven shines,
And often is his gold complexion dimmed;
And every fair from fair sometimes declines,
By chance, or nature's changing course, untrimmed.

Fair = beauty, or more than beauty?

Summer is fleeting and not always perfect. (But lover is perfect?)

But thy eternal summer shall not fade,
Nor lose possession of that fair thou ow'st
Nor shall death brag thou wand'rest in his shade,
When in eternal lines to time thou grow'st.

What are "eternal lines to time"? Ask in class?

Death would be proud to claim the lover but can't?

So long as men can breathe or eyes can see,
So long lives this, and this gives life to thee.

Final couplet seems to signal a shift in thought.

This = the poem? (Art, like the writer's love, is eternal.)

NOTE TAKING ON A LITERARY WORK

Notes on Chrysanthemums.doc - Microsoft Word

File   Edit   View   Insert   Format   Tools   Table   Window   Help

Times New Roman ▾ 14 ▾ **B** *I* U̲ ▤ ▤ ▤ ▤▾ ▤ ✎ ▾ A ▾   » Fi

---

Notes on "Chrysanthemums"

Eliza's gardening clothes—"clodhopper" shoes and a dress "covered by a big corduroy apron"—not very feminine.

The words "strong," "strength," "power," and "powerful" pop up in connection with Eliza and her gardening. Why?

Conversation with pots-and-pans repairman about growing chrysanthemums is sexually charged—"Her breast swelled passionately."

Is she attracted to the traveling repairman or just his way of life? She envies his freedom to sleep outdoors in his wagon: "I wish women could do such things."

Bathtub scene after repairman leaves—awakened sexuality, romance.

What do chrysanthemums symbolize? Beauty? Femininity? Source of pride? Strength? All of these?

Eliza sees chrysanthemums tossed into a ditch. Disillusion.

Taking notes

Note taking is also an important part of rereading a work of literature. In your notes you can try out ideas and develop your perspective on the work. Here are some notes one student took on a short story, "Chrysanthemums," by John Steinbeck. Notice that some of these notes pose questions for further thought.

Discussing the work

As you may have discovered, class discussions can lead to interesting insights about a literary work, perhaps by calling attention to details that you failed to notice on a first reading. Discussions don't always need to occur face-to-face. In many classes, they happen online in discussion forums, chat rooms, blogs, or wikis. On page L-6, for example, is a set of blog postings about a character in Joyce Carol Oates's short story "Where Are You Going, Where Have You Been?"

CONVERSATION ABOUT A SUBJECT

Dr. Connolly's Blog | ENG 101, Section 4

❶ Who is Arnold Friend?
Posted by **Professor Barbara Connolly**, Thu Mar 4, 2010 4:36 PM

At one point during the story Arnold Friend demands, "Don't you know who I am?" Who do you think he is? Does the reader or Connie ever really know?

View comments | Add a comment

---

4 comments on

"Who is Arnold Friend?" Original post

❷ Posted by **Zoe Marshall**, Thu Mar 4, 2010 7:23 PM
I think we're not supposed to know who Arnold Friend is. When he first arrives at Connie's house she asks him, "Who the hell do you think you are?" but Arnold ignores her question by changing the subject. He never tells her who he really is, only that he's her friend and her lover.

Posted by **Mirabel Chavez**, Thu Mar 4, 2010 7:47 PM
Connie is always pretending to be something else to her friends, her boyfriends, and her family. Oates describes her as having two sides: one for home and one for when she's away from home. Pretending is something Connie and Arnold have in common.

Posted by **Jon Fietze**, Thu Mar 4, 2010 8:04 PM
I found a lot of parallels between Arnold and the wolf in "Little Red Riding Hood." For example, Connie notices Arnold's hair, his teeth, and his grin. It reminded me of that part in "Little Red Riding Hood" when Little Red says, "Oh, Grandmother, what big teeth you have!"

Posted by **Yuko Yoshikawa**, Thu Mar 4, 2010 11:11 PM
I was thinking the same thing. Plus, Arnold seems like he's dressing up to hide who he is. Connie thinks that his hair is like a wig, and later that his face is a mask. It reminded me of when the wolf puts on the grandmother's clothing to trick Little Red Riding Hood, just like Arnold is trying to trick Connie.

---

1   Instructor's prompt.
2   A series of student responses to the prompt.

L1-b Form an interpretation.

After rereading, jotting notes, and perhaps discussing the work, you
are ready to start forming an interpretation. At this stage, try to focus
on a single aspect of the work. Look through your notes and annotations for recurring questions and insights related to the aspect you
have chosen.

Focusing on a central issue

In forming an interpretation, you should try to focus on a central
issue. Your job is not to say everything about the work that can possibly be said. It is to develop a sustained, in-depth interpretation that
illuminates the work in some specific way. You may think, for example, that *Huckleberry Finn* is an interesting book because it not only
contains humor and brilliant descriptions of scenery but also tells
a serious story of one boy's coming of age. But to develop this general response into an interpretation, you will have to find a focus. For
example, you might address the ways in which the runaway slave
Jim uses humor to preserve his dignity. Or you might examine the
ironic contradictions between what Huck says and what his heart
tells him.

Asking questions that lead to an interpretation

Good interpretations generally arise from good questions. What is it
about the work that puzzles, intrigues, or unsettles you? What do you
want to know more about? What are you uncertain about? By asking
yourself such questions, you will push yourself to move beyond your
first impressions to deeper insights and better ideas.

Some interpretations answer questions about literary tech-
niques, such as the writer's handling of plot, setting, and character.
Others respond to questions about social context as well—what a
work reveals about the time and culture in which it was written. Both
kinds of questions are included in the chart that begins on page L-8.

Often you will find yourself writing about both technique and social
context. For example, Margaret Peel, a student who wrote about Langston Hughes's poem "Ballad of the Landlord" (see p. L-26), addressed the
following question, which touches on both language and race:

> How does the poem's language—through its four voices—dramatize the
> experience of a black man in a society dominated by whites?

Questions to ask about literature

Questions about technique

Plot. What central conflicts drive the plot? Are they internal (within a character) or external (between characters or between a character and a force)? How are conflicts resolved? Why are events revealed in a particular order?

Setting. Does the setting (time and place) create an atmosphere, give an insight into a character, suggest symbolic meanings, or hint at the theme of the work?

Character. What seems to motivate the central characters? Do any characters change significantly? If so, what—if anything—have they learned from their experiences? Do sharp contrasts between characters highlight important themes?

Point of view. Does the point of view—the perspective from which the story is narrated or the poem is spoken—influence our understanding of events? Does the narration reveal the character of the speaker, or does the speaker merely observe others? Is the narrator perhaps innocent, naive, or deceitful?

Theme. Does the work have an overall theme (a central insight about people or a truth about life, for example)? If so, how do details in the work serve to illuminate this theme?

Language. Does language—such as formal or informal, standard or dialect, prosaic or poetic, cool or passionate—reveal the character of speakers? How do metaphors, similes, and sensory images contribute to the work? How do recurring images enrich the work and hint at its meaning? To what extent do sentence rhythms and sounds underscore the writer's meaning?

Questions about social context

Historical context. What does the work reveal about—or how was it shaped by—the time and place in which it was written? Does the work appear to promote or undermine a philosophy that was popular in its time, such as social Darwinism in the late nineteenth century or the women's movement in the mid-twentieth century?

Class. How does social class shape or influence characters' choices and actions? How does class affect the way characters view—or are viewed by—others? What economic struggles or power relationships does the work reflect or depict?

Race and culture. Are any characters portrayed as being caught between cultures: between the culture of home and the culture of work or school, for example, or between a traditional and an emerging culture? Are any characters engaged in a conflict with society because of their race or ethnic background? To what extent does the work celebrate a specific culture and its traditions?

Gender. Are any characters' choices restricted because of gender? What are the power relationships between the sexes, and do these change during the course of the work? Do any characters resist the gender roles society has assigned to them? Do other characters choose to conform to those roles?

Archetypes (or universal types). Does a character, an image, or a plot fit a pattern—or type—that has been repeated in stories throughout history and across cultures? (For example, nearly every culture has stories about heroes, quests, redemption, and revenge.) How does an archetypal character, image, or plot line correspond to or differ from others like it?

In the introduction of your paper, you will usually announce your interpretation in a one- or two-sentence thesis. The thesis answers the central question that you posed. Here, for example, is Margaret Peel's two-sentence thesis:

> Langston Hughes's "Ballad of the Landlord" is narrated through four voices, each with its own perspective on the poem's action. These opposing voices—of a tenant, a landlord, the police, and the press—dramatize a black man's experience in a society dominated by whites.

L2 Planning the paper

L2-a Draft a thesis.

When planning your paper, it is good to have a working or preliminary thesis in mind. This preliminary thesis will reflect the current state of your thinking about the work and will likely change and evolve as you plan and draft. (See the sections on thesis statements in your handbook.)

In its final form, your thesis will address the central question you asked about the work. It will likely appear at the end of your introduction and will announce your essay's main point. When drafting your thesis, aim for a strong, assertive summary of your interpretation. On page L-10, for example, are two successful thesis statements taken from student essays, together with the central question each student had posed.

QUESTION

What does Emily Dickinson's poem "I dwell in Possibility—" tell us about the writing of poetry?

THESIS

Emily Dickinson's poem "I dwell in Possibility—" implies that poetry itself is limitless and that the role of the poet is not to create poetry but to inhabit and shape it.

QUESTION

What is the significance of the explorer Robert Walton in Mary Shelley's novel *Frankenstein*?

THESIS

Through the character of Walton, Shelley suggests that the most profound sort of knowledge is not a knowledge of nature's secrets but a knowledge of the limits of knowledge itself.

As in other writing, the thesis of a literature paper should not be too factual, too broad, or too vague (see also "thesis" in your handbook). For an essay on Mark Twain's *Huckleberry Finn*, for example, the following would all make poor thesis statements.

TOO FACTUAL

As a runaway slave, Jim is in danger from the law.

TOO BROAD

In *Huckleberry Finn*, Twain criticizes mid-nineteenth-century American society.

TOO VAGUE

Huckleberry Finn is Twain's most exciting work.

The following thesis statement is sharply focused and presents a central idea that requires discussion and support. It connects a general point (that Twain objects to empty piety) to those specific aspects of the novel the paper will address (Huck's status as narrator, Huck's comments on religion).

ACCEPTABLE THESIS

Because Huckleberry Finn is a naive narrator, his comments on conventional religion function ironically at every turn, allowing Twain to poke fun at empty piety.

L2-b Sketch an outline.

Your thesis may strongly suggest a method of organization, in which case you will have little difficulty jotting down your essay's key points. Consider, for example, the following informal outline, based on a thesis that leads naturally to a three-part organization.

Thesis: In Zora Neale Hurston's novel *Their Eyes Were Watching God*, Janie grows into independence through a series of marriages: first to Logan Killicks, who treats her as a source of farm labor; next to Jody Starks, who sees her as a symbol of his own power; and then to Tea Cake, with whom she shares a passionate and satisfying love that leads her to self-discovery.

—Marriage to Logan Killicks: arranged by grandmother, Janie as labor, runs away
—Marriage to Jody Starks: Eatonville, Jody as mayor, violence, Jody's death
—Marriage to Tea Cake: younger man, love, shooting, return to Eatonville

If your thesis does not by itself suggest a method of organization, turn to your notes and begin putting them into categories that relate to the thesis. For example, one student who was writing about Euripides's play *Medea* constructed the following formal outline from her notes.

Thesis: Although Medea professes great love for her children, Euripides gives us reason to doubt her sincerity: Medea does not hesitate to use the children as weapons in her bloody battle with Jason, and from the outset she displays little real concern for their fate.

  I. From the beginning of the play, Medea is a less than ideal mother.
   A. Her first words about the children are hostile.
   B. Her first actions suggest indifference.
  II. In three scenes Medea appears to be a loving mother, but in each of these scenes we have reason to doubt her sincerity.
  III. Throughout the play, as Medea plots her revenge, her overriding concern is not her children but her reputation.
   A. Fearing ridicule, she is proud of her reputation as one who can "help her friends and hurt her enemies."
   B. Her obsession with reputation may stem from the Greek view of reputation as a means of immortality.
  IV. After she kills her children, Medea reveals her real concern.
   A. She shows no remorse.
   B. She revels in Jason's agony over their death.

Whether to use a formal or an informal outline is to some extent a matter of personal preference. For most purposes, you will probably find that an informal outline is sufficient, perhaps even preferable. (See also "outlines" in your handbook.)

☰ **L3** Writing the paper

L3-a Draft an introduction that announces your interpretation.

The introduction to a literature paper is usually one paragraph long. In most cases, you will want to begin the paragraph with a few sentences that provide context for your thesis and to end it with a thesis that sums up your interpretation. You may also want to note the question or issue that motivated your interpretation. In this way, you will help your reader understand not only what your idea or thesis *is* but also why it *matters*.

The following is an introductory paragraph announcing a student's interpretation of one aspect of the novel *Frankenstein*; the thesis is highlighted.

> In Mary Shelley's novel *Frankenstein*, Walton's ambition as an explorer, to find a passage to the North Pole, mirrors Frankenstein's ambition as a scientist, to discover and master the secret of life. But where Frankenstein is ultimately destroyed by his quest for knowledge, Walton turns back from his quest when he learns of Frankenstein's fate. Walton's story might seem unimportant, but paired with Frankenstein's, it keeps us from missing one of the novel's most important themes. Through Walton, Shelley suggests that the most profound and useful sort of knowledge is not a knowledge of nature's secrets but a knowledge of the limits of knowledge itself.

L3-b Support your interpretation with evidence from the work; avoid simple plot summary.

Your thesis and preliminary outline will point you toward details in the work relevant to your interpretation. As you begin drafting the body of your paper, make good use of those details.

Supporting your interpretation

As a rule, each paragraph in the body of your paper should focus on some aspect of your overall interpretation and should include a topic sentence that states the main idea of the paragraph. (See also "topic sentence" in your handbook.) The rest of the paragraph should present details and perhaps quotations from the work that back up your interpretation. In the following paragraph, which develops part of the outline sketched on page L-11, the topic sentence comes first. It sums up the significance of Janie's marriage to Logan Killicks in Zora Neale Hurston's novel *Their Eyes Were Watching God*.

> Janie finds her marriage to Logan Killicks unsatisfying because she did not choose him and cannot love him. The marriage is arranged by Janie's grandmother and caretaker, Nanny, so that Janie will have a secure home after Nanny dies. When Janie objects to the marriage, Nanny tells her, "'Tain't Logan Killicks Ah wants you to have, baby, it's protection" (15). Janie marries Logan even though she does not love him. She "wait[s] for love to begin" (22), but love never comes. At first, Logan dotes on Janie, but as time passes, he demands more and more work from her. Although she works hard in the kitchen, he wants her to perform traditionally masculine tasks such as chopping wood, plowing fields, and shoveling manure. When Janie suggests that they each have their roles—"Youse in yo' place and Ah'm in mine"—Logan asserts his authority over her and doesn't seem to relate to her as family: "You ain't got no particular place. It's wherever Ah need yuh" (31). As husband and wife, Janie and Logan are estranged from each other. Janie tells him, "You ain't done me no favor by marryin' me" (31). To escape this loveless and demeaning marriage, Janie runs away with Joe Starks.

Notice that the writer has quoted dialogue from the novel to lend both flavor and substance to her interpretation (quotations are cited with page numbers). Notice too that the writer is *interpreting* the work: She is not merely summarizing the plot.

Avoiding simple plot summary

In a literature paper, it is tempting to rely heavily on plot summary and avoid interpretation. You can resist this temptation by paying special attention to your topic sentences. The following rough-draft topic sentence, for instance, led to a plot summary rather than an interpretation.

> As they drift down the river on a raft, Huck and the runaway slave Jim have many philosophical discussions.

The student's revised topic sentence, which announces an interpretation, is much better.

> The theme of dawning moral awareness is reinforced by the many philosophical discussions between Huck and Jim, the runaway slave, as they drift down the river on a raft.

Usually a little thought and preparation can make the difference between a plot summary that cannot be developed and a focused, forceful interpretation. As with all writing, revision is key. To avoid simple plot summary, keep the following strategies in mind as you write.

- When you write for an academic audience, you can assume that readers have read the work. You may need to include some summary as background, but the emphasis should be on your ideas about the work.
- Pose questions that lead to an interpretation or judgment of the work rather than to a summary. The questions in the chart that begins on page L-8 can help steer you away from summary and toward interpretation.
- Read your essay out loud. If you hear yourself listing events from the work, stop and revise.
- Rather than organizing your paper according to the work's sequence of events, organize it in a way that brings out the relationships among your ideas.

L4 Observing the conventions of literature papers

The academic discipline of English literature has certain conventions, or standard practices, that scholars in the field use when writing about literature. These conventions help scholars communicate their ideas clearly and efficiently. If you adhere to these conventions, you will enhance your credibility and enable your readers to focus more easily on your ideas.

L4-a Refer to authors, titles, and characters according to convention.

The first time you refer to an author of a literary work or a secondary source, such as a critical essay, use the author's full name: *Virginia Woolf is known for her experimental novels*. In subsequent references, you may use the last name only: *Woolf's early work was largely overlooked*. As a rule, do not use personal titles such as *Mr.* or *Ms.* or *Dr.* when referring to authors.

When you mention the title of a short story, an essay, or a short or medium-length poem, put the title in quotation marks.

"The Progress of Love," by Alice Munro

"Coming Home Again," by Chang-Rae Lee

"Promises like Pie-Crust," by Christina Rossetti

Italicize the titles of novels, nonfiction books, plays, and long poems.

The Poisonwood Bible, by Barbara Kingsolver

I Know Why the Caged Bird Sings, by Maya Angelou

M. Butterfly, by David Henry Hwang

Howl, by Allen Ginsberg

Refer to each character by the name most often used for him or her in the work. If, for instance, a character's name is Lambert Strether and he is always referred to as "Strether," do not call him "Lambert" or "Mr. Strether." Similarly, write "Lady Macbeth," not "Mrs. Macbeth."

L4-b Use the present tense to describe fictional events.

Perhaps because fictional events have not actually occurred in the past, the literary convention is to describe them in the present tense. Until you become used to this convention, you may find yourself shifting between present and past tense. As you revise your draft, make sure that you have used the present tense consistently.

INCONSISTENT USE OF TENSES

Octavia <u>demands</u> blind obedience from James and from all of her children. When James and Ty <u>caught</u> two redbirds in their trap, they <u>wanted</u> to play with them; Octavia, however, <u>had</u> other plans for the birds (89-90).

CONSISTENT USE OF THE PRESENT TENSE

Octavia <u>demands</u> blind obedience from James and from all of her children. When James and Ty <u>catch</u> two redbirds in their trap, they <u>want</u> to play with them; Octavia, however, <u>has</u> other plans for the birds (89-90).

NOTE: When integrating quotations from the work into your own text, you will need to be alert to the problem of shifting tenses. See L5-c.

L4-c Use MLA style to format passages quoted from the work.

Unless your instructor suggests otherwise, use MLA (Modern Language Association) style for formatting passages quoted from literary works.

MLA style usually requires that you name the author of the work quoted and give a page number for the exact location of the passage in the work. When writing about nonfiction articles and books, introduce a quotation with a signal phrase naming the author (*John Smith points out that "...*") or place the author's name and page number in parentheses at the end of the quoted passage: "*..." for all time (Smith 22)*.

When writing about a single work of fiction, however, you do not need to include the author's name each time you quote from the work. You will mention the author's name in the introduction to your paper. Then, when you are quoting from the work, you may include just the page number in parentheses following the quotation (see p. L-20). You may, of course, use the author's name in a signal phrase to highlight the author's role or technique (see p. L-19), but you are not required to do so. (See also L5-a.)

Additional MLA guidelines for handling citations in the text of your paper appear in L5.

L5 Integrating quotations from the work

Integrating quotations from a literary work can lend vivid support to your argument, but keep most quotations fairly short. You can use long quotations to present extended passages you will discuss at length, but use them sparingly. Excessive use of long quotations may interrupt the flow of your interpretation, making your paper more difficult to read and understand.

Integrating quotations smoothly into your own text can present a challenge. Because of the complexities of literature, do not be surprised to find yourself puzzling over the most graceful way to tuck in a short phrase or the clearest way to introduce a more extended passage from the work.

L5-a Do not confuse the work's author with a narrator, speaker, or character.

When introducing quotations from a literary work, make sure that you don't confuse the author with the narrator of a story, the speaker of a poem, or a character in a story or play. Instead of naming the author, you can refer to the narrator or speaker—or to the work itself.

INAPPROPRIATE

Poet Andrew Marvell describes his fear of death like this: "But at my back I always hear / Time's wingèd chariot hurrying near" (21-22).

APPROPRIATE

Addressing his beloved in an attempt to win her sexual favors, the speaker of the poem argues that death gives them no time to waste: "But at my back I always hear / Time's wingèd chariot hurrying near" (21-22).

APPROPRIATE

The poem "To His Coy Mistress" says as much about fleeting time and death as it does about sexual passion. Its most powerful lines are "But at my back I always hear / Time's wingèd chariot hurrying near" (21-22).

In the last example, you could mention the author as well: *Marvell's poem "To His Coy Mistress" says as much.* . . . Although the author is mentioned, readers will not confuse him with the speaker of the poem.

L5-b Provide context for quotations.

When you quote the words of a narrator, speaker, or character in a literary work, you should name who is speaking and provide a context for the quoted words. In the following examples, the quoted dialogue is from Tennessee Williams's play *The Glass Menagerie* and Shirley Jackson's short story "The Lottery."

Laura is so completely under Amanda's spell that when urged to make a wish on the moon, she asks, "What shall I wish for, Mother?" (1.5.140).

When a neighbor suggests that the lottery should be abandoned, Old Man Warner responds, "There's *always* been a lottery" (284).

L5-c As you integrate quotations, avoid shifts in tense.

Because it is conventional to write about literature in the present tense (see L4-b) and because literary works often use other tenses, you will need to exercise some care when weaving quotations into your own writing. One student's first draft of a paper on Nadine Gordimer's short story "Friday's Footprint" included the following awkward sentence, in which the present-tense main verb *sees* is followed by the past-tense verb *blushed* in the quotation.

TENSE SHIFT

When Rita sees Johnny's relaxed attitude, "she blushed, like a wave of illness" (159).

When revising, the writer considered two ways to avoid the distracting shift from present to past tense: to paraphrase the reference to Rita's blushing and reduce the length of the quotation or to change the verb in the quotation to the present tense, using brackets to indicate the change.

REVISION 1

When Rita sees Johnny's relaxed attitude, she is overcome with embarrassment, "like a wave of illness" (159).

REVISION 2

When Rita sees Johnny's relaxed attitude, "she blushe[s], like a wave of illness" (159).

Using brackets around just one letter of a word can seem fussy, so the writer chose the first revision. (See also L5-d.)

L5-d To indicate changes in a quotation, use brackets and the ellipsis mark.

Two marks of punctuation, square brackets and the ellipsis mark (three spaced periods), show readers that you have modified a quoted passage in some way.

Brackets are used for additions, as in the following example from a paper on Khaled Hosseini's novel *A Thousand Splendid Suns*.

Laila, fearful, confides in Tariq: "It's the whistling, the damn whistling [of the rockets], I hate more than anything" (156).

Because some readers might not understand the meaning of *whistling*
out of context, the writer has supplied a clarification in brackets. Brackets are also used to change words or letters to keep a quoted sentence
grammatical in your context, as in the last example in L5-c, or to change
a capital letter to lowercase or vice versa, as on page L-23.

The ellipsis mark is used to indicate omissions. In the following example from a paper on Tim O'Brien's "How to Tell a True War
Story," the writer has omitted some words from the original in order
to keep the quoted passage brief.

> O'Brien warns his readers bluntly that they should not seek noble themes in war
> stories: "If at the end of a war story you feel uplifted, . . . then you have been
> made the victim of a very old and terrible lie" (347).

If you want to omit one or more full sentences from a quotation,
use a period before the three ellipsis dots.

> O'Brien regards war as fundamentally immoral: "A true war story is never moral. . . .
> If a story seems moral, do not believe it" (347).

Usually you do not need an ellipsis mark at the beginning or at
the end of a quotation. But if you have dropped words at the end of the
final quoted sentence, put three ellipsis dots before the closing quotation
mark and parenthetical reference, as in the example on page L-23.

Remember to use brackets and ellipsis marks sparingly. The pur-
pose of quoting is to show your readers the actual language of the
work. Excessive alterations can undermine a quotation's effectiveness
as evidence.

L5-e Enclose embedded quotations in single quotation marks.

In writing about literature, you may sometimes want to use a
quotation with another quotation embedded in it—when you are
quoting dialogue in a novel, for example. In such cases, set off the
main quotation with double quotation marks, as you usually would,
and set off the embedded quotation with single quotation marks. The
following example from a student paper quotes lines from Amy Tan's
novel *The Hundred Secret Senses*.

> Early in the novel the narrator's half-sister Kwan sees—or thinks she sees—ghosts:
> "'Libby-ah,' she'll say to me. 'Guess who I see yesterday, you guess.' And I don't
> have to guess that she's talking about someone dead" (3).

L5-f Use MLA style to cite passages from the work.

MLA guidelines for citing quotations differ somewhat for short stories or novels, poems, and plays.

Short stories or novels

To cite a passage from a short story or a novel, use a page number in parentheses after the quoted words.

> The narrator of Madeleine Thien's "Simple Recipes" remembers a conversation with her mother in which the mother described guilt as something one could "shrink" and "compress." After a time, according to the mother, "you can blow it off your body like a speck of dirt" (12).

If a novel has numbered divisions, give the page number and a semicolon; then indicate the book, part, or chapter in which the passage is found. Use abbreviations such as "bk." and "ch."

> White relies on past authors to help retell the legend of King Arthur. The narrator does not provide specifics about Lancelot's tournament at Corbin, instead telling readers, "If you want to read about the Corbin tournament, Malory has it" (489; bk. 3, ch. 39).

When a quotation from a work of fiction takes up four or fewer typed lines, put it in quotation marks and run it into the text of your essay, as in the two previous examples. When a quotation is five lines or longer, set it off from the text by indenting one inch from the left margin; when you set a quotation off from the text, do not use quotation marks. Put the parenthetical citation after the final mark of punctuation.

> Sister's tale begins with "I," and she makes every event revolve around herself, even her sister's marriage:
>
>> I was getting along fine with Mama, Papa-Daddy and Uncle Rondo until my sister Stella-Rondo just separated from her husband and came back home again. Mr. Whitaker! Of course I went with Mr. Whitaker first, when he first appeared here in China Grove, taking "Pose Yourself" photos, and Stella-Rondo broke us up. (88)

Poems

To cite lines from a poem, use line numbers in parentheses at the end of the quotation. For the first reference, use the word "lines": (lines 1-2). Thereafter, use just the numbers: (12-13).

> The opening lines of Frost's "Fire and Ice" strike a conversational tone: "Some say the world will end in fire, / Some say in ice" (1-2).

Enclose quotations of three or fewer lines of poetry in quotation marks within your text, and indicate line breaks with a slash, as in the example just given.

When you quote four or more lines of poetry, set the quotation off from the text by indenting one inch, and omit the quotation marks. Put the line numbers in parentheses after the final mark of punctuation.

> In the second stanza of "A Noiseless Patient Spider," Whitman turns the spider's weaving into a metaphor for the activity of the human soul:
>
>> And you O my soul where you stand,
>>
>> Surrounded, detached, in measureless oceans of space,
>>
>> Ceaselessly musing, venturing, throwing, seeking the spheres
>>> to connect them,
>>
>> Till the bridge you will need be form'd, till the ductile anchor
>>> hold,
>>
>> Till the gossamer thread you fling catch somewhere, O my
>>> soul. (6-10)

NOTE: If any line of the poem takes up more than one line of your paper, carry the extra words to the next line of the paper and indent them an additional one-quarter inch, as in the previous example. Alternatively, you may indent the entire poem a little less than one inch to fit the long line.

Plays

To cite lines from a play, include the act number, scene number, and line numbers (as many of these as are available) in parentheses at the end of the quotation. Separate the numbers with periods, and use arabic numerals unless your instructor prefers roman numerals.

> Two attendants silently watch as the sleepwalking Lady Macbeth struggles with her conscience: "Here's the smell of the blood still. All the perfumes of Arabia will not sweeten this little hand" (5.1.50-51).

If no act, scene, or line numbers are available, use a page number.

When a quotation from a play takes up four or fewer typed lines in your paper and is spoken by only one character, put quotation marks around it and run it into the text of your essay, as in the previous example. If the quotation consists of two or three lines from a verse play, use a slash for line breaks, as for poetry (see p. L-20). When a quotation by a single character in a play is five typed lines or longer (or more than three lines in a verse play), indent it one inch from the left margin and omit quotation marks. Include the citation in parentheses after the final mark of punctuation.

> Speaking to Electra, Clytemnestra complains about the sexual double standard that has allowed her husband to justify sacrificing her other daughter, Iphigenia, to the gods. She asks what would have happened if Menelaus, and not his wife Helen, had been seized by the Trojans:
>
>> If Menelaus had been raped from home on the sly, should I have had to kill Orestes so my sister's husband could be rescued? You think your father would have borne it? He would have killed me. Then why was it fair for him to kill what belonged to me and not be killed? (1041-45)

When quoting dialogue between two or more characters in a play, no matter how many lines you use, set the quotation off from the text. Type each character's name in all capital letters at a one-inch indent from the left margin. Indent subsequent lines under the character's name an additional one-quarter inch.

> In the opening act of *Translations*, Friel pointedly contrasts the monolingual Captain Lancey with the multilingual Irish:
>
>> HUGH. . . . [Lancey] then explained that he does not speak Irish. Latin? I asked. None. Greek? Not a syllable. He speaks—on his own admission—only English; and to his credit he seemed suitably verecund—James?
>>
>> JIMMY. *Verecundus*—humble.
>>
>> HUGH. Indeed—he voiced some surprise that we did not speak his language. (act 1)

☰ **L6** Using secondary sources

Many literature papers rely wholly on primary sources—the literary work or works under discussion. You document such papers with MLA in-text citations as explained in L5-f. If a list of works cited is required, it will consist of the literary work or works (see L6-a).

In addition to relying on primary sources, some literature papers draw on secondary sources: articles or books of literary criticism, biographies of the author, the author's own essays or autobiography, or histories of the era in which the work was written. When you use secondary sources, you must document them with MLA in-text citations and a list of works cited as explained in L6-a. (For an example of a paper that uses secondary sources, see pp. L-30 to L-35.)

Keep in mind that even when you use secondary sources, your main goal should be to develop and communicate your own understanding and interpretation of the literary work.

L6-a Use MLA style to document secondary sources.

Most literature papers use the documentation system recommended by the Modern Language Association (MLA), as set forth in the *MLA Handbook for Writers of Research Papers*, 7th ed. (New York: MLA, 2009). (For complete details, see the MLA documentation sections in your handbook.)

MLA recommends in-text citations that refer readers to a list of works cited. An in-text citation names the author of the source, often in a signal phrase, and gives the page number in parentheses. At the end of the paper, a list of works cited provides publication information about the sources used in the paper.

MLA IN-TEXT CITATION

Finding Butler's science fiction novel *Xenogenesis* more hopeful than *Frankenstein*, Theodora Goss and John Paul Riquelme note that "[h]uman and creature never bridge their differences in Shelley's narrative, but in Butler's they do . . ." (437).

The signal phrase names the authors of the secondary source; the number in parentheses is the page on which the quoted words appear.

The in-text citation is used in combination with a list of works cited at the end of the paper. Anyone interested in knowing additional information about the secondary source can consult the list of works cited. Here, for example, is the works cited entry for the work referred to in the sample in-text citation.

ENTRY IN THE LIST OF WORKS CITED

Goss, Theodora, and John Paul Riquelme. "From Superhuman to Posthuman: The Gothic Technological Imaginary in Mary Shelley's *Frankenstein* and Octavia Butler's *Xenogenesis*." *Modern Fiction Studies* 53.3 (2007): 434-59. Print.

As you document secondary sources with in-text citations and a list of works cited, you will need to consult the MLA documentation sections in your handbook.

L6-b Avoid plagiarism.

The rules about plagiarism are the same for literature papers as for other research writing. To be fair and ethical, you must acknowledge your debt to the writers of any sources you use. If you don't, you commit plagiarism, a serious academic offense.

In general, three different acts are considered plagiarism: (1) failing to cite quotations and borrowed ideas, (2) failing to enclose borrowed language in quotation marks, and (3) failing to put summaries and paraphrases in your own words. You may want to check out your school's plagiarism policy if you are unfamiliar with it.

If an interpretation was suggested to you by a critic's work or if an obscure point was clarified by someone else's research, it is your responsibility to cite the source (as explained in L6-a). In addition to citing the source, you must place any borrowed language in quotation marks. In the following example, the plagiarized words are underlined.

ORIGINAL SOURCE

Here again Glaspell's story reflects a larger truth about the lives of rural women. Their isolation induced madness in many. The rate of insanity in rural areas, especially for women, was a much-discussed subject in the second half of the nineteenth century.
— Elaine Hedges, "Small Things Reconsidered: 'A Jury of Her Peers,'" p. 59

PLAGIARISM

Glaspell may or may not want us to believe that Minnie Wright's murder of her husband is an insane act, but Minnie's loneliness and isolation certainly could have driven her mad. As Elaine Hedges notes, the rate of insanity in rural areas, especially for women, was a much-discussed subject in the second half of the nineteenth century (59).

BORROWED LANGUAGE IN QUOTATION MARKS

Glaspell may or may not want us to believe that Minnie Wright's murder of her husband is an insane act, but Minnie's loneliness and isolation certainly could have driven her mad. As Elaine Hedges notes, "The rate of insanity in rural areas, especially for women, was a much-discussed subject in the second half of the nineteenth century" (59).

Sometimes writers plagiarize unintentionally because they have difficulty paraphrasing a source's ideas. In the first paraphrase of the following source, the writer has copied the underlined words (without quotation marks) and followed the sentence structure of the source too closely, merely plugging in synonyms (*prowess* for *skill*, *respect* for *esteem*, and so on).

ORIGINAL SOURCE

Mothers [in the late nineteenth century] were advised to teach their daughters to make small, exact stitches, not only for durability but as a way of instilling habits of patience, neatness, and diligence. But such stitches also became a badge of one's needlework skill, a source of self-esteem and of status, through the recognition and admiration of other women.

—Elaine Hedges, "Small Things Reconsidered: 'A Jury of Her Peers,'" p. 62

PLAGIARISM: UNACCEPTABLE BORROWING

One of the final clues in the story, the irregular stitching in Minnie's quilt patches, connects immediately with Mrs. Hale and Mrs. Peters. In the late nineteenth century, explains Elaine Hedges, <u>small, exact stitches</u> were valued <u>not only for</u> their <u>durability</u>. They <u>became a badge of one's</u> prowess with the needle, <u>a source</u> <u>of self-</u>respect <u>and of</u> prestige, <u>through the recognition and</u> approval <u>of other</u> <u>women</u> (62).

ACCEPTABLE PARAPHRASE

One of the final clues in the story, the irregular stitching in Minnie's quilt patches, connects immediately with Mrs. Hale and Mrs. Peters. In the late nineteenth century, explains Elaine Hedges, precise needlework was valued for more than its strength. It was a source of pride to women, a way of gaining status in the community of other women (62).

Although the acceptable version uses a few words found in the original source, it does not borrow entire phrases without quotation marks or closely mimic the structure of the original. To write an acceptable paraphrase, resist the temptation to look at the source while you write; instead, write from memory. When you write from memory, you will be more likely to use your own words. Ask yourself, "What is the author's meaning?" and then in your own words, state your understanding of the author's basic point.

L7 Sample papers

Following are two sample essays. The first, by Margaret Peel, has no secondary sources. (Langston Hughes's "Ballad of the Landlord," the poem on which the essay is based, appears on p. L-29.) The second essay, by Dan Larson, uses secondary sources. (The short story on which the paper is based begins on p. L-36.)

Margaret Peel

Professor Lin

English 102

20 April 2010

Opposing Voices in "Ballad of the Landlord"

Langston Hughes's "Ballad of the Landlord" is narrated through

four voices, each with its own perspective on the poem's action. These

opposing voices—of a tenant, a landlord, the police, and the press—

dramatize a black man's experience in a society dominated by whites.

The main voice in the poem is that of the tenant, who, as the

last line tells us, is black. The tenant is characterized by his informal,

nonstandard speech. He uses slang ("Ten Bucks"), contracted words

(*'member, more'n*), and nonstandard grammar ("These steps is broken

down"). This colloquial English suggests the tenant's separation from the

world of convention, represented by the formal voices of the police and the

press, which appear later in the poem.

Although the tenant uses nonstandard English, his argument is

organized and logical. He begins with a reasonable complaint and a

gentle reminder that the complaint is already a week old: "My roof has

sprung a leak. / Don't you 'member I told you about it / Way last

week?" (lines 2-4). In the second stanza, he appeals diplomatically to the

landlord's self-interest: "These steps is broken down. / When you come up

yourself / It's a wonder you don't fall down" (6-8). In the third stanza,

when the landlord has responded to his complaints with a demand for rent

money, the tenant becomes more forceful, but his voice is still reasonable:

"Ten Bucks you say is due? / Well, that's Ten Bucks more'n I'll pay you / Till

you fix this house up new" (10-12).

The fourth stanza marks a shift in the tone of the argument. At this

point the tenant responds more emotionally, in reaction to the landlord's

threats to evict him. By the fifth stanza, the tenant has unleashed his

anger: "Um-huh! You talking high and mighty" (17). Hughes uses an

exclamation point for the first time; the tenant is raising his voice at last.

As the argument gets more heated, the tenant finally resorts to the

language of violence: "You ain't gonna be able to say a word / If I land

my fist on you" (19-20).

Thesis states Peel's main idea.

Details from the poem illustrate Peel's point.

The first citation for lines of the poem includes the word "lines." Subsequent citations from the poem are cited with line numbers alone.

Topic sentence focuses on an interpretation.

Marginal annotations indicate MLA-style formatting and effective writing.

Peel 2

These are the last words the tenant speaks in the poem. Perhaps Hughes wants to show how black people who threaten violence are silenced. When a new voice is introduced—the landlord's—the poem shifts to a frantic tone:

> *Police! Police!*
> *Come and get this man!*
> *He's trying to ruin the government*
> *And overturn the land!* (21-24)

This response is clearly an overreaction to a small threat. Instead of dealing with the tenant directly, the landlord shouts for the police. His hysterical voice—marked by repetitions and punctuated with exclamation points— reveals his disproportionate fear and outrage. And his conclusions are equally excessive: this black man, he claims, is out to "ruin the government" and "overturn the land." Although the landlord's overreaction is humorous, it is sinister as well, because the landlord knows that, no matter how excessive his claims are, he has the police and the law on his side.

In line 25, the regular meter and rhyme of the poem break down, perhaps showing how an arrest disrupts everyday life. The "voice" in lines 25-29 has two parts: the clanging sound of the police ("Copper's whistle! / Patrol bell!") and, in sharp contrast, the unemotional, factual tone of a police report ("Arrest. / Precinct Station. / Iron cell.").

The last voice in the poem is the voice of the press, represented in newspaper headlines: "MAN THREATENS LANDLORD / TENANT HELD NO BAIL / JUDGE GIVES NEGRO 90 DAYS IN COUNTY JAIL" (31-33). Meter and rhyme return here, as if to show that once the tenant is arrested, life can go on as usual. The language of the press, like that of the police, is cold and distant, and it gives the tenant less and less status. In line 31, he is a "man"; in line 32, he has been demoted to a "tenant"; and in line 33, he has become a "Negro," or just another statistic.

By using four opposing voices in "Ballad of the Landlord," Hughes effectively dramatizes different views of minority assertiveness. To the tenant, assertiveness is informal and natural, as his language shows; to the landlord, it is a dangerous threat, as his hysterical response suggests. The police response is, like the language that describes it, short and sharp. Finally, the press's view of events, represented by the headlines, is

---

Marginal notes:

Transition prepares readers for the next topic.

Peel interprets the landlord's response.

Peel shows how meter and rhyme support the poem's meaning.

Peel sums up her interpretation.

distant and unsympathetic.

Peel concludes with an analysis of the poem's political significance.

  By the end of the poem, we understand the predicament of the black man. Exploited by the landlord, politically oppressed by those who think he's out "to ruin the government," physically restrained by the police and the judicial system, and denied his individuality by the press, he is saved only by his own sense of humor. The very title of the poem suggests his— and Hughes's—sense of humor. The tenant is singing a *ballad* to his oppressors, but this ballad is no love song. It portrays the oppressors, through their own voices, in an unflattering light: the landlord as cowardly and ridiculous, the police and press as dull and soulless. The tenant may lack political power, but he speaks with vitality, and no one can say he lacks dignity or the spirit to survive.

Ballad of the Landlord

LANGSTON HUGHES

Landlord, landlord,
My roof has sprung a leak.
Don't you 'member I told you about it
Way last week?

Landlord, landlord,
These steps is broken down.
When you come up yourself
It's a wonder you don't fall down.

Ten Bucks you say I owe you?
Ten Bucks you say is due?
Well, that's Ten Bucks more'n I'll pay you
Till you fix this house up new.

What? You gonna get eviction orders?
You gonna cut off my heat?
You gonna take my furniture and
Throw it in the street?

Um-huh! You talking high and mighty.
Talk on—till you get through.
You ain't gonna be able to say a word
If I land my fist on you.

Police! Police!
Come and get this man!
He's trying to ruin the government
And overturn the land!

Copper's whistle!
Patrol bell!
Arrest.

Precinct Station.
Iron cell.
Headlines in press:

MAN THREATENS LANDLORD
TENANT HELD NO BAIL
JUDGE GIVES NEGRO 90 DAYS IN COUNTY JAIL

Larson 1

Dan Larson

Professor Duncan

English 102

19 April 2010

The Transformation of Mrs. Peters:

An Analysis of "A Jury of Her Peers"

In Susan Glaspell's 1917 short story "A Jury of Her Peers," two women accompany their husbands and a county attorney to an isolated house where a farmer named John Wright has been choked to death in his bed with a rope. The chief suspect is Wright's wife, Minnie, who is in jail awaiting trial. The sheriff's wife, Mrs. Peters, has come along to gather some personal items for Minnie, and Mrs. Hale has joined her. Early in the story, Mrs. Hale sympathizes with Minnie and objects to the way the male investigators are "snoopin' round and criticizin'" her kitchen (191). In contrast, Mrs. Peters shows respect for the law, saying that the men are doing "no more than their duty" (191). By the end of the story, however, Mrs. Peters has joined Mrs. Hale in a conspiracy of silence, lied to the men, and committed a crime—hiding key evidence. What causes this dramatic change?

One critic, Leonard Mustazza, argues that Mrs. Hale recruits Mrs. Peters "as a fellow 'juror' in the case, moving the sheriff's wife away from her sympathy for her husband's position and towards identification with the accused wom[a]n" (494). While this is true, Mrs. Peters also reaches insights on her own. Her observations in the kitchen lead her to understand Minnie's grim and lonely plight as the wife of an abusive farmer, and her identification with both Minnie and Mrs. Hale is strengthened as the men conducting the investigation trivialize the lives of women.

The first evidence that Mrs. Peters reaches understanding on her own surfaces in the following passage:

> The sheriff's wife had looked from the stove to the sink—
> to the pail of water which had been carried in from
> outside. . . . That look of seeing into things, of seeing
> through a thing to something else, was in the eyes of the
> sheriff's wife now. (194)

Something about the stove, the sink, and the pail of water connects with

---

The opening lines name the story and establish context.

Present tense is used to describe details from the story.

Quotations from the story are cited with page numbers in parentheses.

The opening paragraph ends with Larson's research question.

The thesis asserts Larson's main point.

A long quotation is set off by indenting; no quotation marks are needed; ellipsis dots indicate a sentence omitted from the source.

Larson 2

her own experience, giving Mrs. Peters a glimpse into the life of Minnie Wright. The details resonate with meaning.

Social historian Elaine Hedges argues that such details, which evoke the drudgery of a farm woman's work, would not have been lost upon Glaspell's readers in 1917. Hedges tells us what the pail and the stove, along with another detail from the story—a dirty towel on a roller—would have meant to women of the time. Laundry was a dreaded all-day affair. Water had to be pumped, hauled, and boiled; then the wash was rubbed, rinsed, wrung through a wringer, carried outside, and hung on a line to dry. "What the women see, beyond the pail and the stove," writes Hedges, "are the hours of work it took Minnie to produce that one clean towel" (56).

On her own, Mrs. Peters discovers clues about the motive for the murder. Her curiosity leads her to pick up a sewing basket filled with quilt pieces and then to notice something strange: a sudden row of badly sewn stitches. "What do you suppose she was so—nervous about?" asks Mrs. Peters (195). A short time later, Mrs. Peters spots another clue, an empty birdcage. Again she observes details on her own, in this case a broken door and hinge, suggesting that the cage has been roughly handled.

In addition to noticing details, both women draw conclusions from them and speculate on their significance. When Mrs. Hale finds the dead canary beneath a quilt patch, for example, the women conclude that its neck has been wrung and understand who must have wrung it.

As the women speculate on the significance of the dead canary, each connects the bird with her own experience. Mrs. Hale knows that Minnie once sang in the church choir, an activity that Mr. Wright put a stop to, just as he put a stop to the bird's singing. Also, as a farmer's wife, Mrs. Hale understands the desolation and loneliness of life on the prairie. She sees that the bird was both a thing of beauty and a companion. "If there had been years and years of—nothing, then a bird to sing to you," says Mrs. Hale, "it would be awful—still—after the bird was still" (198). To Mrs. Peters, the stillness of the canary evokes memories of the time when she and her husband homesteaded in the northern plains. "I know what stillness is," she says, as she recalls the death of her first child, with no one around to console her (198).

Larson summarizes ideas from a secondary source and then quotes from that source; he names the author in a signal phrase and gives a page number in parentheses.

Topic sentences present Larson's interpretation.

Details from the story provide evidence for the interpretation.

Elaine Hedges has written movingly of the isolation that women experienced on late-nineteenth- and early-twentieth-century farms of the West and Midwest:

> Women themselves reported that it was not unusual to spend five months in a log cabin without seeing another woman . . . or to spend one and a half years after arriving before being able to take a trip to town . . . . (54)

To combat loneliness and monotony, says Hedges, many women bought canaries and hung the cages outside their sod huts. The canaries provided music and color, a "spot of beauty" that "might spell the difference between sanity and madness" (60).

Mrs. Peters and Mrs. Hale understand—and Glaspell's readers in 1917 would have understood—what the killing of the bird means to Minnie. For Mrs. Peters, in fact, the act has a special significance. When she was a child, a boy axed her kitten to death and, as she says, "If they hadn't held me back I would have . . . hurt him" (198). She has little difficulty comprehending Minnie's murderous rage, for she has felt it herself.

Although Mrs. Peters's growing empathy for Minnie stems largely from her observations, it is also prompted by her negative reaction to the patronizing comments of the male investigators. At several points in the story, her body language reveals her feelings. For example, when Mr. Hale remarks that "women are used to worrying over trifles," both women move closer together and remain silent. When the county attorney asks, "for all their worries, what would we do without the ladies?" the women do not speak, nor do they "unbend" (190). The fact that the women respond in exactly the same way reveals the extent to which they are bonding.

Both women are annoyed at the way in which the men criticize and trivialize the world of women. The men question the difficulty of women's work. For example, when the county attorney points to the dirty towel on the rack as evidence that Minnie wasn't much of a housekeeper, Mrs. Hale replies, "There's a great deal of work to be done on a farm" (190). Even the importance of women's work is questioned. The men kid the women for trying to decide if Minnie was going to quilt or knot patches together for a quilt and laugh about such trivial concerns. Those very

Ellipsis dots indicate omitted words within the sentence and at the end of the sentence.

Transition serves as a bridge from one section of the paper to the next.

Larson 4

quilts, of course, kept the men warm at night and cost them nothing
beyond the price of thread.

The men also question the women's wisdom and intelligence. For
example, when the county attorney tells the women to keep their eyes out
for clues, Mr. Hale replies, "But would the women know a clue if they did
come upon it?" (191). The women's response is to stand motionless and
silent. The irony is that the men don't see the household clues that are
right in front of them.

By the end of the story, Mrs. Peters has been so transformed that she
risks lying to the men. When the county attorney walks into the kitchen
and notices the birdcage the women have found, he asks about the
whereabouts of the bird. Mrs. Hale replies, "We think the cat got it" (197),
even though she knows from Mrs. Peters that Minnie was afraid of cats and
would not have owned one. Instead of correcting the lie, Mrs. Peters
elaborates on it, saying of cats, "They're superstitious, you know; they
leave" (198). Clearly Mrs. Hale is willing to risk lying because she is
confident that Mrs. Peters won't contradict her.

Larson gives evidence that Mrs. Peters has been transformed.

The Mrs. Peters character may have been based on a real sheriff's
wife. Seventeen years before writing "A Jury of Her Peers," Susan Glaspell
covered a murder case for the *Des Moines Daily News*. A farmer's wife,
Margaret Hossack, was accused of murdering her sleeping husband with two
axe blows to the head. In one of her newspaper reports, Glaspell wrote that
the sheriff's wife sat next to Mrs. Hossack and "frequently applied her
handkerchief to her eyes" (qtd. in Ben-Zvi 30).

Larson draws on a secondary source that gives background on Glaspell's life.

We do not know from the short story the ultimate fate of Minnie
Wright, but Margaret Hossack, whose case inspired the story, was found
guilty, though the case was later thrown out by the Iowa Supreme Court.
However, as Linda Ben-Zvi points out, the women's guilt or innocence is
not the issue:

> Whether Margaret Hossack or Minnie Wright committed
> murder is moot; what is incontrovertible is the brutality
> of their lives, the lack of options they had to redress
> grievances or to escape abusive husbands, and the
> complete disregard of their plight by the courts and by
> society. (38)

Larson 5

These are the issues that Susan Glaspell wished to stress in "A Jury of Her
Peers."

Larson's conclusion
echoes his main
point without dully
repeating it.

These are also the issues that Mrs. Peters comes to understand as the
story unfolds, with her understanding deepening as she identifies with
Minnie and Mrs. Hale and is repulsed by male attitudes. Her transformation
becomes complete when the men joke that she is "married to the law" and
she responds by violating the law: hiding key evidence, the dead canary.

Larson 6

Works Cited

Ben-Zvi, Linda. "'Murder, She Wrote': The Genesis of Susan Glaspell's
      Trifles." *Theatre Journal* 44.2 (1992): 141–62. Rpt. in *Susan
      Glaspell: Essays on Her Theater and Fiction*. Ed. Linda Ben-Zvi.
      Ann Arbor: U of Michigan P, 1995. 19-48. Print.

Glaspell, Susan. "A Jury of Her Peers." *Literature and Its Writers: A
      Compact Introduction to Fiction, Poetry, and Drama*. Ed. Ann
      Charters and Samuel Charters. 5th ed. Boston: Bedford, 2010.
      185-201. Print.

Hedges, Elaine. "Small Things Reconsidered: 'A Jury of Her Peers.'"
      Women's Studies 12.1 (1986): 89-110. Rpt. in *Susan Glaspell:
      Essays on Her Theater and Fiction*. Ed. Linda Ben-Zvi. Ann
      Arbor: U of Michigan P, 1995. 49-69. Print.

Mustazza, Leonard. "Generic Translation and Thematic Shift in Susan
      Glaspell's *Trifles* and 'A Jury of Her Peers.'" *Studies in Short
      Fiction* 26.4 (1989): 489-96. Print.

The works cited
page lists the
primary source
(Glaspell's story) and
secondary sources.

A Jury of Her Peers

SUSAN GLASPELL

When Martha Hale opened the storm-door and got a cut of the north wind, she ran back for her big woolen scarf. As she hurriedly wound that round her head her eye made a scandalized sweep of her kitchen. It was no ordinary thing that called her away—it was probably further from ordinary than anything that had ever happened in Dickson County. But what her eye took in was that her kitchen was in no shape for leaving: her bread all ready for mixing, half the flour sifted and half unsifted.

She hated to see things half done; but she had been at that when the team from town stopped to get Mr. Hale, and then the sheriff came running in to say his wife wished Mrs. Hale would come too—adding, with a grin, that he guessed she was getting scary and wanted another woman along. So she had dropped everything right where it was.

"Martha!" now came her husband's impatient voice. "Don't keep folks waiting out here in the cold."

She again opened the storm-door, and this time joined the three men and the one woman waiting for her in the big two-seated buggy.

After she had the robes tucked around her she took another look at the woman who sat beside her on the back seat. She had met Mrs. Peters the year before at the county fair, and the thing she remembered about her was that she didn't seem like a sheriff's wife. She was small and thin and didn't have a strong voice. Mrs. Gorman, sheriff's wife before Gorman went out and Peters came in, had a voice that somehow seemed to be backing up the law with every word. But if Mrs. Peters didn't look like a sheriff's wife, Peters made it up in looking like a sheriff. He was to a dot the kind of man who could get himself elected sheriff—a heavy man with a big voice, who was particularly genial with the law-abiding, as if to make it plain that he knew the difference between criminals and non-criminals. And right there it came into Mrs. Hale's mind, with a stab, that this man who was so pleasant and lively with all of them was going to the Wrights' now as a sheriff.

"The country's not very pleasant this time of year," Mrs. Peters at last ventured, as if she felt they ought to be talking as well as the men.

Mrs. Hale scarcely finished her reply, for they had gone up a little hill and could see the Wright place now, and seeing it did not make her feel like talking. It looked very lonesome this cold March morning. It had always been a lonesome-looking place. It was down in a hollow, and the poplar trees around it were lonesome-looking trees. The men were looking at it and talking about what had happened. The county attorney was bending to one side of the buggy, and kept looking steadily at the place as they drew up to it.

"I'm glad you came with me," Mrs. Peters said nervously, as the two women were about to follow the men in through the kitchen door.

Even after she had her foot on the door-step, her hand on the knob, Martha Hale had a moment of feeling she could not cross that threshold. And the reason it seemed she couldn't cross it now was simply because she hadn't crossed it before. Time and time again it had been in her mind, "I ought to go over and see Minnie Foster"—she still thought of her as Minnie Foster, though for twenty years she had been Mrs. Wright. And then there was always something to do and Minnie Foster would go from her mind. But *now* she could come.

The men went over to the stove. The women stood close together by the door. Young Henderson, the county attorney, turned around and said, "Come up to the fire, ladies."

Mrs. Peters took a step forward, then stopped. "I'm not—cold," she said.

And so the two women stood by the door, at first not even so much as looking around the kitchen.

The men talked for a minute about what a good thing it was the sheriff had sent his deputy out that morning to make a fire for them, and then Sheriff Peters stepped back from the stove, unbuttoned his outer coat, and leaned his hands on the kitchen table in a way that seemed to mark the beginning of official business. "Now, Mr. Hale," he said in a sort of semi-official voice, "before we move things about, you tell Mr. Henderson just what it was you saw when you came here yesterday morning."

The county attorney was looking around the kitchen.

"By the way," he said, "has anything been moved?" He turned to the sheriff. "Are things just as you left them yesterday?"

Peters looked from cupboard to sink; from that to a small worn rocker a little to one side of the kitchen table.

"It's just the same."

"Somebody should have been left here yesterday," said the county attorney.

"Oh—yesterday," returned the sheriff, with a little gesture as of yesterday having been more than he could bear to think of. "When I had to send Frank to Morris Center for that man who went crazy—let me tell you. I had my hands full *yesterday*. I knew you could get back from Omaha by today, George, and as long as I went over everything here myself —"

"Well, Mr. Hale," said the county attorney, in a way of letting what was past and gone go, "tell just what happened when you came here yesterday morning."

Mrs. Hale, still leaning against the door, had that sinking feeling of the mother whose child is about to speak a piece. Lewis often wandered along and got things mixed up in a story. She hoped he would tell this straight and plain, and not say unnecessary things that would just make things harder for Minnie Foster. He didn't begin at once, and she noticed that he looked queer—as if standing in that kitchen and having to tell what he had seen there yesterday morning made him almost sick.

"Yes, Mr. Hale?" the county attorney reminded.

"Harry and I had started to town with a load of potatoes," Mrs. Hale's husband began.

Harry was Mrs. Hale's oldest boy. He wasn't with them now, for the very good reason that those potatoes never got to town yesterday and he was taking them this morning, so he hadn't been home when the sheriff stopped to say he wanted Mr. Hale to come over to the Wright place and tell the county attorney his story there, where he could point it all out. With all Mrs. Hale's other emotions came the fear now that maybe Harry wasn't dressed warm enough—they hadn't any of them realized how that north wind did bite.

"We come along this road," Hale was going on, with a motion of his hand to the road over which they had just come, "and as we got in sight of the house I says to Harry, 'I'm goin' to see if I can't get John Wright to take a telephone.' You see," he explained to Henderson, "unless I can get somebody to go in with me they won't come out this branch road except for a price I can't pay. I'd spoke to Wright about it once before; but he put me off, saying folks talked too much anyway, and all he asked was peace and quiet—guess you know about how much he talked himself. But I thought maybe if I went to the house and talked about it before his wife, and said all the women-folks liked the telephones, and that in this lonesome stretch of road it would be a good thing—well, I said to Harry that that was what I was going to say—though I said at the same time that I didn't know as what his wife wanted made much difference to John —"

Now there he was!—saying things he didn't need to say. Mrs. Hale tried to catch her husband's eye, but fortunately the county attorney interrupted with:

"Let's talk about that a little later, Mr. Hale. I do want to talk about that, but I'm anxious now to get along to just what happened when you got here."

When he began this time, it was very deliberately and carefully:

"I didn't see or hear anything. I knocked at the door. And still it was all quiet inside. I knew they must be up—it was past eight o'clock. So I knocked again, louder, and I thought I heard somebody say, 'Come in.' I wasn't sure—I'm not sure yet. But I opened the door—this door," jerking a hand toward the door by which the two women stood, "and there, in that rocker"—pointing to it—"sat Mrs. Wright."

Everyone in the kitchen looked at the rocker. It came into Mrs. Hale's mind that that rocker didn't look in the least like Minnie Foster—the Minnie Foster of twenty years before. It was a dingy red, with wooden rungs up the back, and the middle rung was gone, and the chair sagged to one side.

"How did she—look?" the county attorney was inquiring.

"Well," said Hale, "she looked—queer."

"How do you mean—queer?"

As he asked it he took out a note-book and pencil. Mrs. Hale did not like the sight of that pencil. She kept her eye fixed on her husband, as if to keep him from saying unnecessary things that would go into that note-book and make trouble.

Hale did speak guardedly, as if the pencil had affected him too.

"Well, as if she didn't know what she was going to do next. And kind of—done up."

"How did she seem to feel about your coming?"

"Why, I don't think she minded—one way or other. She didn't pay much attention. I said, 'Ho' do, Mrs. Wright? It's cold, ain't it?' And she said, 'Is it?'—and went on pleatin' at her apron.

"Well, I was surprised. She didn't ask me to come up to the stove, or to sit down, but just set there, not even lookin' at me. And so I said: 'I want to see John.'

"And then she—laughed. I guess you would call it a laugh.

"I thought of Harry and the team outside, so I said, a little sharp, 'Can I see John?' 'No,' says she—kind of dull like. 'Ain't he home?' says I. Then she looked at me. 'Yes,' says she, 'he's home.' 'Then why can't I see him?' I asked her, out of patience with her now. 'Cause he's dead' says she, just as quiet and dull—and fell to pleatin' her apron. 'Dead?' says I, like you do when you can't take in what you've heard.

"She just nodded her head, not getting a bit excited, but rockin' back and forth.

"'Why—where is he?' says I, not knowing what to say.

"She just pointed upstairs—like this"—pointing to the room above.

"I got up, with the idea of going up there myself. By this time I—didn't know what to do. I walked from there to here; then I says: 'Why, what did he die of?'

"'He died of a rope around his neck,' says she; and just went on pleatin' at her apron."

Hale stopped speaking, and stood staring at the rocker, as if he were still seeing the woman who had sat there the morning before. Nobody spoke; it was as if every one were seeing the woman who had sat there the morning before.

"And what did you do then?" the county attorney at last broke the silence.

"I went out and called Harry. I thought I might—need help. I got Harry in, and we went upstairs." His voice fell almost to a whisper. "There he was—lying over the —"

"I think I'd rather have you go into that upstairs," the county attorney interrupted, "where you can point it all out. Just go on now with the rest of the story."

"Well, my first thought was to get that rope off. It looked —"

He stopped, his face twitching.

"But Harry, he went up to him, and he said, 'No, he's dead all right, and we'd better not touch anything.' So we went downstairs.

"She was still sitting that same way. 'Has anybody been notified?' I asked. 'No,' says she, unconcerned. "'Who did this, Mrs. Wright?' said Harry. He said it businesslike, and she stopped pleatin' at her apron. 'I don't know,' she says. 'You don't *know*?' says Harry. 'Weren't you sleepin' in the bed with him?' 'Yes,' says she, 'but I was on the inside.' 'Somebody slipped a rope round his neck and strangled him, and you didn't wake up?' says Harry. 'I didn't wake up,' she said after him.

"We may have looked as if we didn't see how that could be, for after a minute she said, 'I sleep sound.'

"Harry was going to ask her more questions, but I said maybe that weren't our business; maybe we ought to let her tell her story first to the coroner or the sheriff. So Harry went fast as he could over to High Road—the Rivers' place, where there's a telephone."

"And what did she do when she knew you had gone for the coroner?" The attorney got his pencil in his hand all ready for writing.

"She moved from that chair to this one over here"—Hale pointed to a small chair in the corner—"and just sat there with her hands held together and looking down. I got a feeling that I ought to make some conversation, so I said I had come in to see if John wanted to put in a telephone; and at that she started to laugh, and then she stopped and looked at me—scared."

At the sound of a moving pencil the man who was telling the story looked up.

"I dunno—maybe it wasn't scared," he hastened: "I wouldn't like to say it was. Soon Harry got back, and then Dr. Lloyd came, and you, Mr. Peters, and so I guess that's all I know that you don't."

He said that last with relief, and moved a little, as if relaxing. Everyone moved a little. The county attorney walked toward the stair door.

"I guess we'll go upstairs first—then out to the barn and around there."

He paused and looked around the kitchen.

"You're convinced there was nothing important here?" he asked the sheriff. "Nothing that would—point to any motive?"

The sheriff too looked all around, as if to re-convince himself.

"Nothing here but kitchen things," he said, with a little laugh for the insignificance of kitchen things.

The county attorney was looking at the cupboard—a peculiar, ungainly structure, half closet and half cupboard, the upper part of it being built in the wall, and the lower part just the old-fashioned kitchen cupboard. As if its queerness attracted him, he got a chair and opened the upper part and looked in. After a moment he drew his hand away sticky.

"Here's a nice mess," he said resentfully.

The two women had drawn nearer, and now the sheriff's wife spoke.

"Oh—her fruit," she said, looking to Mrs. Hale for sympathetic understanding. She turned back to the county attorney and explained: "She worried about that when it turned so cold last night. She said the fire would go out and her jars might burst."

Mrs. Peters' husband broke into a laugh.

"Well, can you beat the woman! Held for murder, and worrying about her preserves!"

The young attorney set his lips.

"I guess before we're through with her she may have something more serious than preserves to worry about."

"Oh, well," said Mrs. Hale's husband, with good-natured superiority, "women are used to worrying over trifles."

The two women moved a little closer together. Neither of them spoke. The county attorney seemed suddenly to remember his manners—and think of his future.

"And yet," said he, with the gallantry of a young politician, "for all their worries, what would we do without the ladies?"

The women did not speak, did not unbend. He went to the sink and began washing his hands. He turned to wipe them on the roller towel—whirled it for a cleaner place.

"Dirty towels! Not much of a housekeeper, would you say, ladies?"

He kicked his foot against some dirty pans under the sink.

"There's a great deal of work to be done on a farm," said Mrs. Hale stiffly.

"To be sure. And yet"—with a little bow to her—"I know there are some Dickson County farm-houses that do not have such roller towels." He gave it a pull to expose its full length again.

"Those towels get dirty awful quick. Men's hands aren't always as clean as they might be."

"Ah, loyal to your sex, I see," he laughed. He stopped and gave her a keen look. "But you and Mrs. Wright were neighbors. I suppose you were friends, too."

Martha Hale shook her head.

"I've seen little enough of her of late years. I've not been in this house—it's more than a year."

"And why was that? You didn't like her?"

"I liked her well enough," she replied with spirit. "Farmers' wives have their hands full, Mr. Henderson. And then —" She looked around the kitchen.

"Yes?" he encouraged.

"It never seemed a very cheerful place," said she, more to herself than to him.

"No," he agreed; "I don't think anyone would call it cheerful. I shouldn't say she had the home-making instinct."

"Well, I don't know as Wright had, either," she muttered.

"You mean they didn't get on very well?" he was quick to ask.

"No; I don't mean anything," she answered, with decision. As she turned a little away from him, she added: "But I don't think a place would be any the cheerfuller for John Wright's bein' in it."

"I'd like to talk to you about that a little later, Mrs. Hale," he said. "I'm anxious to get the lay of things upstairs now."

He moved toward the stair door, followed by the two men.

"I suppose anything Mrs. Peters does'll be all right?" the sheriff inquired. "She was to take in some clothes for her, you know—and a few little things. We left in such a hurry yesterday."

The county attorney looked at the two women whom they were leaving alone there among the kitchen things.

"Yes—Mrs. Peters," he said, his glance resting on the woman who was not Mrs. Peters, the big farmer woman who stood behind the sheriff's wife. "Of course Mrs. Peters is one of us," he said, in a manner of entrusting responsibility. "And keep your eye out, Mrs. Peters, for anything that might be of use. No telling; you women might come upon a clue to the motive—and that's the thing we need."

Mr. Hale rubbed his face after the fashion of a showman getting ready for a pleasantry.

"But would the women know a clue if they did come upon it?" he said; and, having delivered himself of this, he followed the others through the stair door.

The women stood motionless and silent, listening to the foot-steps, first upon the stairs, then in the room above them.

Then, as if releasing herself from something strange, Mrs. Hale began to arrange the dirty pans under the sink, which the county attorney's disdainful push of the foot had deranged.

"I'd hate to have men comin' into my kitchen," she said testily — "snoopin' round and criticizin'."

"Of course it's no more than their duty," said the sheriff's wife, in her manner of timid acquiescence.

"Duty's all right," replied Mrs. Hale bluffly; "but I guess that deputy sheriff that come out to make the fire might have got a little of this on." She gave the roller towel a pull. "Wish I'd thought of that sooner! Seems mean to talk about her for not having things slicked up, when she had to come away in such a hurry."

She looked around the kitchen. Certainly it was not "slicked up." Her eye was held by a bucket of sugar on a low shelf. The cover was off the wooden bucket, and beside it was a paper bag — half full.

Mrs. Hale moved toward it.

"She was putting this in there," she said to herself — slowly.

She thought of the flour in her kitchen at home — half sifted, half not sifted. She had been interrupted, and had left things half done. What had interrupted Minnie Foster? Why had that work been left half done? She made a move as if to finish it, — unfinished things always bothered her, — and then she glanced around and saw that Mrs. Peters was watching her — and she didn't want Mrs. Peters to get that feeling she had got of work begun and then — for some rea-son — not finished.

"It's a shame about her fruit," she said, and walked toward the cupboard that the county attorney had opened, and got on the chair, murmuring: "I wonder if it's all gone."

It was a sorry enough looking sight, but "Here's one that's all right," she said at last. She held it toward the light. "This is cherries, too." She looked again. "I declare I believe that's the only one."

With a sigh, she got down from the chair, went to the sink, and wiped off the bottle.

"She'll feel awful bad, after all her hard work in the hot weather. I remember the afternoon I put up my cherries last summer."

She set the bottle on the table, and, with another sigh, started to sit down in the rocker. But she did not sit down. Something kept her from sitting down in that chair. She straightened — stepped back, and, half turned away, stood looking at it, seeing the woman who had sat there "pleatin' at her apron."

The thin voice of the sheriff's wife broke in upon her: "I must be getting those things from the front-room closet." She opened the door into the other room, started in, stepped back. "You coming with me, Mrs. Hale?" she asked nervously. "You—you could help me get them."

They were soon back—the stark coldness of that shut-up room was not a thing to linger in.

"My!" said Mrs. Peters, dropping the things on the table and hurrying to the stove.

Mrs. Hale stood examining the clothes the woman who was being detained in town had said she wanted.

"Wright was close!" she exclaimed, holding up a shabby black skirt that bore the marks of much making over. "I think maybe that's why she kept so much to herself. I s'pose she felt she couldn't do her part; and then, you don't enjoy things when you feel shabby. She used to wear pretty clothes and be lively—when she was Minnie Foster, one of the town girls, singing in the choir. But that—oh, that was twenty years ago."

With a carefulness in which there was something tender, she folded the shabby clothes and piled them at one corner of the table. She looked up at Mrs. Peters, and there was something in the other woman's look that irritated her.

"She don't care," she said to herself. "Much difference it makes to her whether Minnie Foster had pretty clothes when she was a girl."

Then she looked again, and she wasn't so sure; in fact, she hadn't at any time been perfectly sure about Mrs. Peters. She had that shrinking manner, and yet her eyes looked as if they could see a long way into things.

"This all you was to take in?" asked Mrs. Hale.

"No," said the sheriff's wife; "she said she wanted an apron. Funny thing to want," she ventured in her nervous little way, "for there's not much to get you dirty in jail, goodness knows. But I suppose just to make her feel more natural. If you're used to wearing an apron—. She said they were in the bottom drawer of this cupboard. Yes—here they are. And then her little shawl that always hung on the stair door."

She took the small gray shawl from behind the door leading upstairs, and stood a minute looking at it.

Suddenly Mrs. Hale took a quick step toward the other woman.

"Mrs. Peters!"

"Yes, Mrs. Hale?"

"Do you think she—did it?"

A frightened look blurred the other thing in Mrs. Peters' eyes.

"Oh, I don't know," she said, in a voice that seemed to shrink away from the subject.

"Well, I don't think she did," affirmed Mrs. Hale stoutly. "Asking for an apron, and her little shawl. Worryin' about her fruit."

"Mr. Peters says—." Footsteps were heard in the room above; she stopped, looked up, then went on in a lowered voice: "Mr. Peters says—it looks bad for her. Mr. Henderson is awful sarcastic in a speech, and he's going to make fun of her saying she didn't—wake up."

For a moment Mrs. Hale had no answer. Then, "Well, I guess John Wright didn't wake up—when they was slippin' that rope under his neck," she muttered.

"No, it's *strange*," breathed Mrs. Peters. "They think it was such a—funny way to kill a man."

She began to laugh; at the sound of the laugh, abruptly stopped.

"That's just what Mr. Hale said," said Mrs. Hale, in a resolutely natural voice. "There was a gun in the house. He says that's what he can't understand."

"Mr. Henderson said, coming out, that what was needed for the case was a motive. Something to show anger—or sudden feeling."

"Well, I don't see any signs of anger around here," said Mrs. Hale, "I don't —" She stopped. It was as if her mind tripped on something. Her eye was caught by a dishtowel in the middle of the kitchen table. Slowly she moved toward the table. One half of it was wiped clean, the other half messy. Her eyes made a slow, almost unwilling turn to the bucket of sugar and the half empty bag beside it. Things begun—and not finished.

After a moment she stepped back, and said, in that manner of releasing herself:

"Wonder how they're finding things upstairs? I hope she had it a little more redd up up there. You know,"—she paused, and feeling gathered,—"it seems kind of *sneaking*: locking her up in town and coming out here to get her own house to turn against her!"

"But, Mrs. Hale," said the sheriff's wife, "the law is the law."

"I s'pose 'tis," answered Mrs. Hale shortly.

She turned to the stove, saying something about that fire not being much to brag of. She worked with it a minute, and when she straightened up she said aggressively:

"The law is the law—and a bad stove is a bad stove. How'd you like to cook on this?"—pointing with the poker to the broken lining. She opened the oven door and started to express her opinion of the oven; but she was swept into her own thoughts, thinking of what it would mean, year after year, to have that stove to wrestle with. The thought of Minnie Foster trying to bake in that oven — and the thought of her never going over to see Minnie Foster — .

She was startled by hearing Mrs. Peters say: "A person gets discouraged — and loses heart."

The sheriff's wife had looked from the stove to the sink — to the pail of water which had been carried in from outside. The two women stood there silent, above them the footsteps of the men who were looking for evidence against the woman who had worked in that kitchen. That look of seeing into things, of seeing through a thing to something else, was in the eyes of the sheriff's wife now. When Mrs. Hale next spoke to her, it was gently:

"Better loosen up your things, Mrs. Peters. We'll not feel them when we go out."

Mrs. Peters went to the back of the room to hang up the fur tippet she was wearing. A moment later she exclaimed, "Why, she was piecing a quilt," and held up a large sewing basket piled high with quilt pieces.

Mrs. Hale spread some of the blocks on the table.

"It's log-cabin pattern," she said, putting several of them together. "Pretty, isn't it?"

They were so engaged with the quilt that they did not hear the footsteps on the stairs. Just as the stair door opened Mrs. Hale was saying:

"Do you suppose she was going to quilt it or just knot it?"

The sheriff threw up his hands.

"They wonder whether she was going to quilt it or just knot it!"

There was a laugh for the ways of women, a warming of hands over the stove, and then the county attorney said briskly:

"Well, let's go right out to the barn and get that cleared up."

"I don't see as there's anything so strange," Mrs. Hale said resentfully, after the outside door had closed on the three men — "our taking up our time with little things while we're waiting for them to get the evidence. I don't see as it's anything to laugh about."

"Of course they've got awful important things on their minds," said the sheriff's wife apologetically.

They returned to an inspection of the block for the quilt. Mrs. Hale was looking at the fine, even sewing, and preoccupied with thoughts of the woman who had done that sewing, when she heard the sheriff's wife say, in a queer tone:

"Why, look at this one."

She turned to take the block held out to her.

"The sewing," said Mrs. Peters, in a troubled way. "All the rest of them have been so nice and even — but — this one. Why, it looks as if she didn't know what she was about!"

Their eyes met—something flashed to life, passed between them; then, as if with an effort, they seemed to pull away from each other. A moment Mrs. Hale sat there, her hands folded over that sewing which was so unlike all the rest of the sewing. Then she had pulled a knot and drawn the threads.

"Oh, what are you doing, Mrs. Hale?" asked the sheriff's wife, startled.

"Just pulling out a stitch or two that's not sewed very good," said Mrs. Hale mildly.

"I don't think we ought to touch things," Mrs. Peters said, a little helplessly.

"I'll just finish up this end," answered Mrs. Hale, still in that mild, matter-of-fact fashion.

She threaded a needle and started to replace bad sewing with good. For a little while she sewed in silence. Then, in that thin, timid voice, she heard:

"Mrs. Hale!"

"Yes, Mrs. Peters?"

"What do you suppose she was so—nervous about?"

"Oh, *I* don't know," said Mrs. Hale, as if dismissing a thing not important enough to spend much time on. "I don't know as she was—nervous. I sew awful queer sometimes when I'm just tired."

She cut a thread, and out of the corner of her eye looked up at Mrs. Peters. The small, lean face of the sheriff's wife seemed to have tightened up. Her eyes had that look of peering into something. But next moment she moved, and said in her thin, indecisive way:

"Well, I must get those clothes wrapped. They may be through sooner than we think. I wonder where I could find a piece of paper—and string."

"In that cupboard, maybe," suggested Mrs. Hale, after a glance around.

One piece of the crazy sewing remained unripped. Mrs. Peters' back turned, Martha Hale now scrutinized that piece, compared it with the dainty, accurate sewing of the other blocks. The difference was startling. Holding this block made her feel queer, as if the distracted thoughts of the woman who had perhaps turned to it to try and quiet herself were communicating themselves to her.

Mrs. Peters' voice roused her.

"Here's a bird-cage," she said. "Did she have a bird, Mrs. Hale?"

"Why, I don't know whether she did or not." She turned to look at the cage Mrs. Peters was holding up. "I've not been here in so long." She sighed. "There was a man round last year selling canaries cheap—but I don't know as she took one. Maybe she did. She used to sing real pretty herself."

Mrs. Peters looked around the kitchen.

"Seems kind of funny to think of a bird here." She half laughed—an attempt to put up a barrier. "But she must have had one—or why would she have a cage? I wonder what happened to it."

"I suppose maybe the cat got it," suggested Mrs. Hale, resuming her sewing.

"No; she didn't have a cat. She's got that feeling some people have about cats—being afraid of them. When they brought her to our house yesterday, my cat got in the room, and she was real upset and asked me to take it out."

"My sister Bessie was like that," laughed Mrs. Hale.

The sheriff's wife did not reply. The silence made Mrs. Hale turn round. Mrs. Peters was examining the bird-cage.

"Look at this door," she said slowly. "It's broke. One hinge has been pulled apart."

Mrs. Hale came nearer.

"Looks as if someone must have been—rough with it."

Again their eyes met—startled, questioning, apprehensive. For a moment neither spoke nor stirred. Then Mrs. Hale, turning away, said brusquely:

"If they're going to find any evidence, I wish they'd be about it. I don't like this place."

"But I'm awful glad you came with me, Mrs. Hale." Mrs. Peters put the bird-cage on the table and sat down. "It would be lonesome for me—sitting here alone."

"Yes, it would, wouldn't it?" agreed Mrs. Hale, a certain determined naturalness in her voice. She had picked up the sewing, but now it dropped in her lap, and she murmured in a different voice: "But I tell you what I *do* wish, Mrs. Peters. I wish I had come over sometimes when she was here. I wish—I had."

"But of course you were awful busy, Mrs. Hale. Your house—and your children."

"I could've come," retorted Mrs. Hale shortly. "I stayed away because it weren't cheerful—and that's why I ought to have come. I"—she looked around—"I've never liked this place. Maybe because it's down in a hollow and you don't see the road. I don't know what it is, but it's a lonesome place, and always was. I wish I had come over to see Minnie Foster sometimes. I can see now —" She did not put it into words.

"Well, you mustn't reproach yourself," counseled Mrs. Peters. "Somehow, we just don't see how it is with other folks till—something comes up."

"Not having children makes less work," mused Mrs. Hale, after a silence, "but it makes a quiet house—and Wright out to work all day—and no company when he did come in. Did you know John Wright, Mrs. Peters?"

"Not to know him. I've seen him in town. They say he was a good man."

"Yes—good," conceded John Wright's neighbor grimly. "He didn't drink, and kept his word as well as most, I guess, and paid his debts. But he was a hard man, Mrs. Peters. Just to pass the time of day with him—." She stopped, shivered a little. "Like a raw wind that gets to the bone." Her eye fell upon the cage on the table before her, and she added, almost bitterly: "I should think she would've wanted a bird!"

Suddenly she leaned forward, looking intently at the cage. "But what do you s'pose went wrong with it?"

"I don't know," returned Mrs. Peters; "unless it got sick and died."

But after she said it she reached over and swung the broken door. Both women watched it as if somehow held by it.

"You didn't know—her?" Mrs. Hale asked, a gentler note in her voice.

"Not till they brought her yesterday," said the sheriff's wife.

"She—come to think of it, she was kind of like a bird herself. Real sweet and pretty, but kind of timid and—fluttery. How—she—did—change."

That held her for a long time. Finally, as if struck with a happy thought and relieved to get back to everyday things, she exclaimed:

"Tell you what, Mrs. Peters, why don't you take the quilt in with you? It might take up her mind."

"Why, I think that's a real nice idea, Mrs. Hale," agreed the sheriff's wife, as if she too were glad to come into the atmosphere of a simple kindness. "There couldn't possibly be any objection to that, could there? Now, just what will I take? I wonder if her patches are in here—and her things?"

They turned to the sewing basket.

"Here's some red," said Mrs. Hale, bringing out a roll of cloth. Underneath that was a box. "Here, maybe her scissors are in here—and her things." She held it up. "What a pretty box! I'll warrant that was something she had a long time ago—when she was a girl."

She held it in her hand a moment; then, with a little sigh, opened it.

Instantly her hand went to her nose.

"Why—!"

Mrs. Peters drew nearer—then turned away.

"There's something wrapped up in this piece of silk," faltered Mrs. Hale.

"This isn't her scissors," said Mrs. Peters, in a shrinking voice.

Her hand not steady, Mrs. Hale raised the piece of silk. "Oh, Mrs. Peters!" she cried. "It's —"

Mrs. Peters bent closer.

"It's the bird," she whispered.

"But, Mrs. Peters!" cried Mrs. Hale. "*Look* at it! Its *neck* — look at its neck! It's all — other side *to.*"

She held the box away from her.

The sheriff's wife again bent closer.

"Somebody wrung its neck," said she, in a voice that was slow and deep.

And then again the eyes of the two women met — this time clung together in a look of dawning comprehension, of growing horror. Mrs. Peters looked from the dead bird to the broken door of the cage. Again their eyes met. And just then there was a sound at the outside door.

Mrs. Hale slipped the box under the quilt pieces in the basket, and sank into the chair before it. Mrs. Peters stood holding to the table. The county attorney and the sheriff came in from outside.

"Well, ladies," said the county attorney, as one turning from serious things to little pleasantries, "have you decided whether she was going to quilt it or knot it?"

"We think," began the sheriff's wife in a flurried voice, "that she was going to — knot it."

He was too preoccupied to notice the change that came in her voice on that last.

"Well, that's very interesting, I'm sure," he said tolerantly. He caught sight of the bird-cage. "Has the bird flown?"

"We think the cat got it," said Mrs. Hale in a voice curiously even.

He was walking up and down, as if thinking something out.

"Is there a cat?" he asked absently.

Mrs. Hale shot a look up at the sheriff's wife.

"Well, not *now*," said Mrs. Peters. "They're superstitious, you know; they leave."

She sank into her chair.

The county attorney did not heed her. "No sign at all of anyone having come in from the outside," he said to Peters, in the manner of continuing an interrupted conversation. "Their own rope. Now let's go upstairs again and go over it, piece by piece. It would have to have been someone who knew just the —"

The stair door closed behind them and their voices were lost.

The two women sat motionless, not looking at each other, but as if peering into something and at the same time holding back. When they spoke now it was as if they were afraid of what they were saying, but as if they could not help saying it.

"She liked the bird," said Martha Hale, low and slowly. "She was going to bury it."

"When I was a girl," said Mrs. Peters, under her breath, "my kitten—there was a boy took a hatchet, and before my eyes—before I could get there —" She covered her face an instant. "If they hadn't held me back I would have"—she caught herself, looked upstairs where footsteps were heard, and finished weakly—"hurt him."

Then they sat without speaking or moving.

"I wonder how it would seem," Mrs. Hale at last began, as if feeling her way over strange ground—"never to have had any children around?" Her eyes made a slow sweep of the kitchen, as if seeing what that kitchen had meant through all the years. "No, Wright wouldn't like the bird," she said after that—"a thing that sang. She used to sing. He killed that too." Her voice tightened.

Mrs. Peters moved uneasily.

"Of course we don't know who killed the bird."

"I knew John Wright," was Mrs. Hale's answer.

"It was an awful thing was done in this house that night, Mrs. Hale," said the sheriff's wife. "Killing a man while he slept—slipping a thing round his neck that choked the life out of him."

Mrs. Hale's hand went out to the bird-cage.

"His neck. Choked the life out of him."

"We don't *know* who killed him," whispered Mrs. Peters wildly. "We don't *know*."

Mrs. Hale had not moved. "If there had been years and years of—nothing, then a bird to sing to you, it would be awful—still—after the bird was still."

It was as if something within her not herself had spoken, and it found in Mrs. Peters something she did not know as herself.

"I know what stillness is," she said, in a queer, monotonous voice. "When we homesteaded in Dakota, and my first baby died—after he was two years old—and me with no other then —"

Mrs. Hale stirred.

"How soon do you suppose they'll be through looking for the evidence?"

"I know what stillness is," repeated Mrs. Peters, in just the same way. Then she too pulled back. "The law has got to punish crime, Mrs. Hale," she said in her tight little way.

"I wish you'd seen Minnie Foster," was the answer, "when she wore a white dress with blue ribbons, and stood up there in the choir and sang."

The picture of that girl, the fact that she had lived neighbor to that girl for twenty years, and had let her die for lack of life, was suddenly more than she could bear.

"Oh, I *wish* I'd come over here once in a while!" she cried. "That was a crime! Who's going to punish that?"

"We mustn't take on," said Mrs. Peters, with a frightened look toward the stairs.

"I might 'a' known she needed help! I tell you, it's *queer*, Mrs. Peters. We live close together, and we live far apart. We all go through the same things—it's all just a different kind of the same thing! If it weren't—why do you and I *understand*? Why do we *know*—what we know this minute?"

She dashed her hand across her eyes. Then, seeing the jar of fruit on the table, she reached for it and choked out:

"If I was you I wouldn't *tell* her her fruit was gone! Tell her it *ain't*. Tell her it's all right—all of it. Here—take this in to prove it to her! She—she may never know whether it was broke or not."

She turned away.

Mrs. Peters reached out for the bottle of fruit as if she were glad to take it—as if touching a familiar thing, having something to do, could keep her from something else. She got up, looked about for something to wrap the fruit in, took a petticoat from the pile of clothes she had brought from the front room, and nervously started winding that round the bottle.

"My!" she began, in a high, false voice, "it's a good thing the men couldn't hear us! Getting all stirred up over a little thing like a—dead canary." She hurried over that. "As if that could have anything to do with—with—My, wouldn't they *laugh*?"

Footsteps were heard on the stairs.

"Maybe they would," muttered Mrs. Hale—"maybe they wouldn't."

"No, Peters," said the county attorney incisively; "it's all perfectly clear, except the reason for doing it. But you know juries when it comes to women. If there was some definite thing—something to show. Something to make a story about. A thing that would connect up with this clumsy way of doing it."

In a covert way Mrs. Hale looked at Mrs. Peters. Mrs. Peters was looking at her. Quickly they looked away from each other. The outer door opened and Mr. Hale came in.

"I've got the team round now," he said. "Pretty cold out there."

"I'm going to stay here awhile by myself," the county attorney suddenly announced. "You can send Frank out for me, can't you?" he asked the sheriff. "I want to go over everything. I'm not satisfied we can't do better."

Again, for one brief moment, the two women's eyes found one another.

The sheriff came up to the table.

"Did you want to see what Mrs. Peters was going to take in?"

The county attorney picked up the apron. He laughed.

"Oh, I guess they're not very dangerous things the ladies have picked out."

Mrs. Hale's hand was on the sewing basket in which the box was concealed. She felt that she ought to take her hand off the basket. She did not seem able to. He picked up one of the quilt blocks which she had piled on to cover the box. Her eyes felt like fire. She had a feeling that if he took up the basket she would snatch it from him.

But he did not take it up. With another little laugh, he turned away, saying:

"No; Mrs. Peters doesn't need supervising. For that matter, a sheriff's wife is married to the law. Ever think of it that way, Mrs. Peters?"

Mrs. Peters was standing beside the table. Mrs. Hale shot a look up at her; but she could not see her face. Mrs. Peters had turned away. When she spoke, her voice was muffled.

"Not—just that way," she said.

"Married to the law!" chuckled Mrs. Peters' husband. He moved toward the door into the front room, and said to the county attorney:

"I just want you to come in here a minute, George. We ought to take a look at these windows."

"Oh—windows," said the county attorney scoffingly.

"We'll be right out, Mr. Hale," said the sheriff to the farmer, who was still waiting by the door.

Hale went to look after the horses. The sheriff followed the county attorney into the other room. Again—for one final moment—the two women were alone in that kitchen.

Martha Hale sprang up, her hands tight together, looking at that other woman, with whom it rested. At first she could not see her eyes, for the sheriff's wife had not turned back since she turned away at that suggestion of being married to the law. But now Mrs. Hale made her turn back. Her eyes made her turn back. Slowly, unwillingly, Mrs. Peters turned her head until her eyes met the eyes of the other woman. There was a moment when they held each other in a steady, burning look in which there was no evasion nor flinching. Then Martha Hale's eyes pointed the way to the basket in which was hidden the thing that would make certain the conviction of the other woman—that woman who was not there and yet who had been there with them all through that hour.

For a moment Mrs. Peters did not move. And then she did it. With a rush forward, she threw back the quilt pieces, got the box, tried to put it in her handbag. It was too big. Desperately she opened it, started to take the bird out. But there she broke—she could not touch the bird. She stood there helpless, foolish.

There was the sound of a knob turning in the inner door. Martha Hale snatched the box from the sheriff's wife, and got it in the pocket of her big coat just as the sheriff and the county attorney came back into the kitchen.

"Well, Henry," said the county attorney facetiously, "at least we found out that she was not going to quilt it. She was going to—what is it you call it, ladies?"

Mrs. Hale's hand was against the pocket of her coat.

"We call it—knot it, Mr. Henderson."

Acknowledgments

Linda Ben-Zvi, excerpt from "'Murder, She Wrote': The Genesis of Susan Glaspell's *Trifles*." *Theatre Journal* 44:2 (1992), 141–62. Copyright © 1992 The Johns Hopkins University Press. Reprinted with permission of The Johns Hopkins University Press.

Brian Friel, excerpt from *Translations* from *Selected Plays of Brian Friel*. Used with permission from The Catholic University of America Press, Washington, D.C.

Robert Frost, excerpt from "Fire and Ice" from *The Poetry of Robert Frost*, edited by Edward Connery Lathem. Copyright 1923, 1939, 1947, © 1967, © 1969 by Henry Holt and Company. Copyright © 1964, 1967, 1970, 1975 by Lesley Frost Ballantine. Copyright 1936, 1942, 1944, 1951, © 1956, 1958 by Robert Frost. Reprinted with the permission of Henry Holt and Company, LLC.

Susan Glaspell, "A Jury of Her Peers," 1917. Copyright © Valentina A. Cook. Used by permission. All rights reserved.

Elaine Hedges, excerpts from "Small Things Reconsidered: Susan Glaspell's 'A Jury of Her Peers'" in *Women's Studies* 12 (1986): 89–110. Copyright © Taylor & Francis, reprinted by permission of the publisher (Taylor & Francis Group, http://www.informaworld.com).

Langston Hughes, "Ballad of the Landlord" from *The Collected Poems of Langston Hughes*, edited by Arnold Rampersad with David Roessel, Associate Editor, Copyright © 1994 by The Estate of Langston Hughes. Used by permission of Alfred A. Knopf, a division of Random House, Inc. and Harold Ober Associates.

Shirley Jackson, excerpt from "The Lottery" from *The Lottery and Other Stories* by Shirley Jackson. Copyright © 1948, 1949 by Shirley Jackson. Copyright renewed 1976, 1977 by Laurence Hyman, Barry Hyman, Mrs. Sarah Webster and Mrs. Joanne Schnurer.

Michael Meyer, question adapted from *The Bedford Introduction to Literature*, Ninth Edition, p. 745. Bedford/St. Martin's, 2010. Copyright © 2010 by Bedford/St. Martin's.

Leonard Mustazza, excerpt from "Generic Translation and Thematic Shift in Susan Glaspell's *Trifles* and 'A Jury of Her Peers'" in *Studies in Short Fiction* 26, no. 4 (Fall, 1989): 489–96. Copyright © 1989 Fayetteville State University.

Tim O'Brien, excerpt from "How to Tell a True War Story" from *The Things They Carried*. Copyright © 1990 by Tim O'Brien. Reprinted by permission of Houghton Mifflin Harcourt Publishing Company and HarperCollins Ltd. All rights reserved.

Amy Tan, excerpt from "The Girl with Yin Eyes" from *The Hundred Secret Senses*. Copyright © 1995 by Amy Tan. Used by permission of G. P. Putnam's Sons, a division of Penguin Group (USA) Inc., the author and the Sandra Dijkstra Literary Agency.

Madeleine Thien, excerpt from "Simple Recipes." Copyright © Madeleine Thien, 2001. Published by McClelland & Stewart Ltd.

Eudora Welty, excerpt from "Why I Live at the P. O." from *A Curtain of Green and Other Stories*, copyright © 1941 and renewed 1969 by Eudora Welty. Reprinted by permission of Houghton Mifflin Harcourt Publishing Company and Russell & Volkening as agents for the author. Originally published by *The Atlantic Monthly*, April 1941.

Index